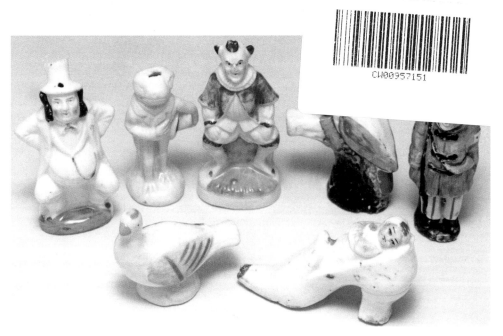

Whistles consisting of continental hard-paste porcelain figures, 1880–1910.

WHISTLES

Martyn Gilchrist

The Shire Book

Published in 2000 by Shire Publications Ltd,
Cromwell House, Church Street, Princes Risborough,
Buckinghamshire HP27 9AA, UK.
(Website: www.shirebooks.co.uk)

British Library Cataloguing in Publication Data:
Gilchrist, Martyn
Whistles. – (The Shire book)
1. Whistles – Collectors and collecting
I. Title 688.7
ISBN 0 7478 0472 9

Cover: *(From back to front) German porcelain mug, 'A present from Minehead', c.1890; continental porcelain bird on a branch, c.1890; Westerwald stoneware bird, twentieth century; A. De Courcy & Co knife-whistle, patent 9499/1905; continental terracotta figure of a boy, c.1900; J. Hudson & Co 'Acme Thunderer' in green 'Acmeoid' (Bakelite), 1910s; Japanese 'penny toy' playing-card, 1930s; silver two-tone whistle, 1894; A. Downing Ltd silver châtelaine mechanical pencil, 1895; J. Dixon & Sons bone pea whistle, 1870s; Victorian jasper with quartz nickel-silver whistle; Smith & Wright, Beaufort whistle, registered design 191579/1892; English porcelain dog's-head whistle, c.1820.*

ACKNOWLEDGEMENTS
The author would like to thank Roger Prebble and Brian Hayes for their help in the
preparation of this book. All the photographs are copyright Martyn Gilchrist. The trade
catalogue illustrated on page 9 is reproduced by permission of Kelham Island Museum,
Sheffield, and that on page 22 by permission of Birmingham Library Services.

NOTE ON THE CAPTIONS
Many patterns of whistles have been made over several years, often decades. The dates in
the captions refer specifically to the whistles illustrated.

Printed in Great Britain by CIT Printing Services Ltd,
Press Buildings, Merlins Bridge, Haverfordwest,
Pembrokeshire SA61 1XF.

Contents

(Top) George Unite Beaufort whistle, 1925; hoof-shaped horn whistle; J. Stevens & Sons, 1860s; cast-silver dog's-head, 1991; S. Auld round pea whistle, 1880s. (Bottom) J. Linegar pea whistle, 1880s; Thomas Yates duck's-head, 1870s; Bent & Parker 'New Borough', patent 10828/1894; G. & J. W. Hawksley engraved domed pea whistle, late nineteenth century; bone two-chambered whistle, early nineteenth century.

Introduction

Whistles made from the bones of birds and other animals have been known since prehistoric times. Throughout history they have been fashioned from materials such as wood, plant stems, horn, ivory, antler, ceramics, many minerals, and several metals and alloys. They have been made in hundreds of different patterns to meet the demands of a large and changing population.

Whistles, also known as calls, are in the same class of instruments as recorders and flageolets, a group which is classified by the way the sound is made. A mouthpiece directs the breath on to the edge of a notch (the *window*) cut into a hollow tube (the *body*), which sets the air within the body vibrating. This vibration is transmitted to the surroundings and is perceived by the ear as sound. The shorter the body the higher the pitch, and a *pea* (cork ball) can modify the sound. Pea whistles were once called 'self tip whistles', implying that the sound was similar to that made by a musician 'tipping', or, in other

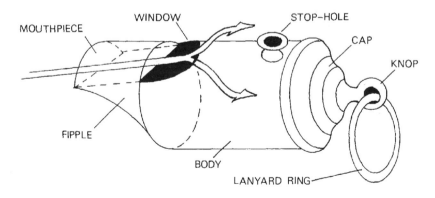

Diagram naming the parts of a round whistle and showing the airflow split by the edge of the window. The vibration of the air within the whistle is transmitted to the surroundings and is perceived by the ear as sound.

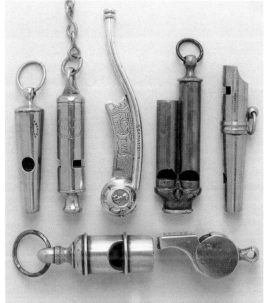

Whistle types. (Top, from left) W. Dowler & Sons Beaufort whistle, 1880s; Bent & Parker general service whistle, 1880s; J. Hudson & Co bosun's call, 1928; J. Hudson & Co multi-tube whistle with in-line mouthpiece, 1885; J. Dixon & Sons composite whistle, 1880s. (Bottom, from left) J. Stevens & Sons round whistle, 1870s; S. Auld escargot, 1890s.

words, producing a series of short separate notes by manipulating the tongue.

Whistles that collectors discover will generally date from not earlier than the end of the eighteenth century and most will date from the 1860s or later. The leading manufacturers during most of the nineteenth century, of whistles employed as signalling instruments, were J. Stevens & Sons of London, J. Dixon & Sons of Sheffield and Thomas Yates of Birmingham. Additionally, during the last quarter of that century four manufacturers from Birmingham – Bent & Parker, W. Dowler & Sons, J. Hudson & Co and A. De Courcy & Co – and the company of S. Auld of Glasgow, were all important makers. There were smaller makers whose whistles are more difficult to find. From Birmingham there were Coney & Co, H. A. Ward, J. Barrall, Smith & Wright, R. A. Walton and J. Linegar. From London there was H. W. Short. There were two from Glasgow, Black & Co and P. McDonald, and two from Sheffield, Hill Bros and G. & J. W. Hawksley. Whistles marked Sykes, a Sheffield company, were possibly made by J. Dixon & Sons. By 1927 J. Hudson & Co of Birmingham had become the most significant producer; the other companies had either ceased trading or were producing few whistles. Adie Bros and Stadium Ltd manufactured in the 1940s and three further companies – M. Y. Dart & Co of Barnet, B & H Whistles of Birmingham and R. Perry & Co (Cosalt) of Birkenhead have been making calls from the second half of the twentieth century.

Several types of whistle have specific names. A **Beaufort** whistle is conical, the narrow end being placed in the mouth. A **general service** whistle is the pattern often referred to as a 'police whistle'. A **bosun's call** consists of a narrow tube leading to a spherical, or barrel-shaped, resonating chamber. An **escargot** is a pea whistle much favoured by railway companies and sports referees, and it is so called as its shape suggests that of a snail. **Round** whistles, with or without a pea, have a single window and the end of the body shaped to form a mouthpiece. A **composite** whistle is one made up from two whistles joined top to top. **Multi-tube** whistles have several separate tubes joined together leading to a single mouthpiece, and **multi-chambered** whistles consist of several chambers within a body.

Whistles in the countryside

Whistle manufacturers have produced for many years a variety of models to meet the desires and tastes of those who enjoy countryside pursuits. They fall into three broad categories: those for professional shepherds; those for use by country lovers generally; and whistles intended to be given as gifts.

Manufacturers have exploited the fact that a dog's ear is most sensitive to high-pitched sounds by aiming their advertisements for sharp-sounding models at dog owners. Makers not only made patterns in metal, but also standard lines in horn, bone and ivory, the natural materials sought after by those having an affection for the countryside. However, such whistles have a drawback: because a dog learns to respond to a particular pitch, if the owner's whistle is lost and a replacement cannot be found that produces a note of identical pitch, the dog needs to be retrained. This problem was solved in two ways:

(Left to right) German, horn; hoof-shaped horn and fur; black antler; J. Dixon & Sons, ivory; J. Hudson & Co, antler, made to a standard pitch.

(Top) Antler, 160 mm. (Bottom, left to right) German, horn with stop-hole; horn shepherd's whistle; J. Hudson & Co 'Acmeoid' (Bakelite), 1930s; J. Hudson & Co two-chambered horn, 1900s.

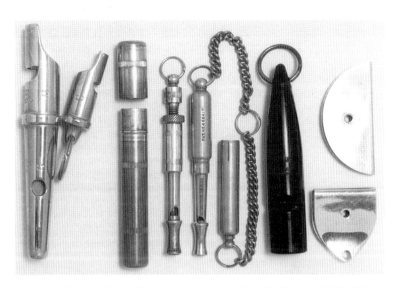

Above: J. Hudson & Co. (Left to right) Shepherd's whistle marked 'G', 'D' and 'C', for 'Go', 'Down' and 'Come', 1960s; silent dog whistle with original case, 1930s; silent dog whistle with integral case, patent 486417/1938; fixed-pitch dog whistle No. 211½, 1970s; (above) shepherd's mouth whistle, nickel silver, 1960s; (below) shepherd's mouth whistle, polished aluminium, 1940s.

Left: (Left) Walking cane with silver band and antler dog's-head whistle, 1934; (right) riding crop.

firstly, by whistles made to an exact pitch, and, secondly, by whistles whose pitch could be set by the purchaser.

J. Hudson & Co produced whistles of the first type in stag horn, and in plastic from the 1960s, accurately tuned to predetermined pitches. Additionally they made three models which consisted of three different fixed-pitch metal whistles joined together and marked with the letters 'G', 'D' and 'C' (signifying 'Go', 'Down' and 'Come'), to which a dog could be trained.

The second type of whistle, that with a variable pitch, falls into two categories: the silent dog whistle and the shepherd's mouth whistle. Professor Sir Francis Galton undertook experiments in the nineteenth century to determine the hearing characteristics of animals and, in particular, dogs. His discovery that dogs could hear sounds beyond the human range led to the silent dog whistle, and a call based on Galton's findings was launched in the early 1930s. The user sets the desired pitch by shortening, or increasing, the effective working length of the whistle by adjusting the height of a rod within the body of the call. The other type of instrument, the mouth whistle, is constructed from an approximately circular piece of metal, or bite-resistant plastic, folded in half with a hole pierced through the top and bottom. It is inserted into the mouth with the open edge outwards, and notes are obtained by manipulating the tongue whilst blowing.

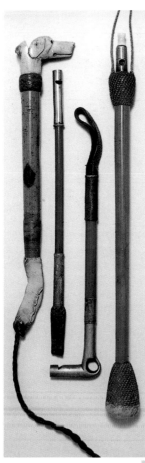

(Left to right) Whip with bone dog's-head whistle, 1910s; cane with 1896 silver whistle, 310 mm; cane with nickel silver whistle and silver band marked 'Swaine'; J. Dixon & Sons lead-weighted cane and whistle with bone mouthpiece, 1880s.

Whistles combined with riding crops are unusual, but several models of dog whips and short canes with whistles were made. In an 1883 catalogue of sporting goods by J. Dixon & Sons two patterns were advertised, and G. & J. W. Hawksley listed four models in 1913. Often the canes and dog whips are stamped with the retailer's or maker's name on a silver or plated band. Whistles were combined with canes which had lead-weighted ends, and with the handles of walking canes for town and country use. J. Dixon & Sons and G. & J. W. Hawksley have accommodated the shooter by merging cartridge extractors, turn-screws, nipple keys and other gun tools with whistles. The most common tool, the cartridge extractor, was also made by several other companies including J. Hudson & Co and A. De Courcy & Co. Patterns by J. Dixon & Sons are the most frequently found and a distinctive feature of some of their whistles is the trumpet and banner trademark or the notched rectangular window with the top corners extending upwards.

There are a large number of calls that have been designed to imitate the sound of a variety of animals. Many of them use reeds and so are not true whistles, but the following calls do

Below: *Late-nineteenth-century shooters' gadgets. (Left to right) J. Dixon & Sons sixteen-gauge extractor (note the notched window with extended top corners); J. Dixon & Sons twelve-gauge extractor with bird-killing blade, Moffatt's patent 11396/1887; J. Dixon & Sons twelve-gauge extractor with turn-screw and nipple key; G. & J. W. Hawksley folding twelve-gauge extractor.*

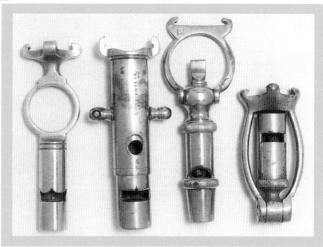

Right: *J. Dixon & Sons. Page 53 of their c.1883 catalogue.*

Below: *Two-chambered whistle stamped 'Sykes', length 50 mm. It is unclear if Sykes of Sheffield ever made whistles and this one is probably by J. Dixon & Sons.*

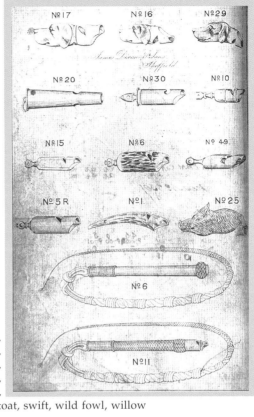

operate as whistles: blackbird, canary, cuckoo, curlew, dove, grouse, guinea fowl, hen (heath, moor and water), jay, lark, mouse, nightingale, oystercatcher, peewit, pheasant, pigeon, plover, quail, redshank, sandpiper, screech owl, skylark, snipe, stoat, swift, wild fowl, willow warbler and woodcock.

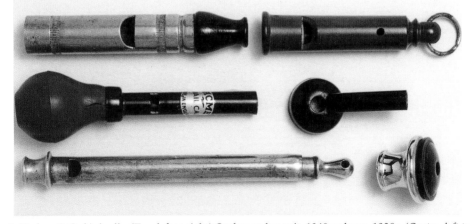

J. Hudson & Co bird calls. (Top, left to right) Curlew and peewit, 1940s; plover, 1930s. (Centre, left to right) Quail, 1930s; snipe, 1940s. (Bottom, left to right) Canary slide whistle, 1930s, length closed 120 mm; general bird effects, 1930s.

Left: *(Back, left to right) J. Hudson & Co all-metal nightingale call with mouthpiece-cover and filler-cap, 1930s; J. Hudson & Co jay call, 1960s. (Centre) French pheasant call. (Front) French concertina-action quail call.*

Right: *Songster, or warbler, whistles that require partial filling with water to operate properly. (Top, left to right) Plated brass; brass, shaped as a smoker's pipe. (Bottom, left to right) Britannia metal; J. Hudson & Co, 1930s.*

Left: *Cuckoo calls. (Top, left to right) J. Hudson & Co, wood, 1910s, length 130 mm; J. Hudson & Co, plastic, 1970s. (Centre, left to right) Wood, top stylised as a bird's head; J. Hudson & Co. (Bottom, left to right) Bird on hazel; Turin, Italy, carved wood, 1900s.*

The nightingale call is unusual as it requires water to operate correctly. It consists of a container quarter-filled with water into which the combined whistle and mouthpiece go. When blown, the whistle can produce wonderful trills and notes. A pattern for the serious user comes with a mouthpiece-cover and a watertight filler-cap, allowing it to be carried without fear of spillage.

Another call of particular interest is the metal, wooden, plastic or ceramic cuckoo call, which has been made with a variety of users in mind – for the serious naturalist, as a souvenir or gift, and as an

Right: *(Left to right) J. Hudson & Co dove or pigeon call, 1960s, length 175 mm; wooden cuckoo effects instrument with sliding top; J. Hudson & Co plated-brass cuckoo effects instrument with sliding wooden top marked with the notes 'G' and 'F', 1930s; J. Hudson & Co plated cuckoo call with sliding top, 1930s.*

Below: *(Back, left to right) Royal Worcester, 1913; continental hard-paste porcelain, c.1900; Wemyss ware, early twentieth century; English porcelain, c.1820. (Front) Continental hard-paste porcelain, c.1900, length 82 mm.*

(Top, left to right) Pressed horn, 1910s, length 70 mm; Thomas Yates nickel silver, 1870; slate. (Bottom, left to right) J. Dixon & Sons, ivory, 1880s; Thomas Yates copper-plated Britannia metal, 1870s; J. Hudson & Co Bakelite, 1930s.

11

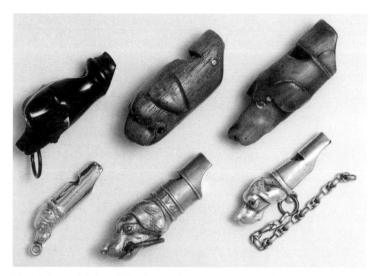

(Top, left to right) Whitby jet; mahogany with ivory fipple; pressed horn. (Bottom, left to right) Gold-plated nickel silver; Thomas Yates, Britannia metal, 1890s, length 48 mm; pressed silver.

orchestral effects instrument. All the calls have either a slideable top or a stop-hole; the effects instruments have both – this permits tuning to an orchestra. A stop-hole is a hole in the body over which a finger may be placed to produce a second note. To make the distinctive cuckoo sound, cover the stop hole, or partially slide out the top, before blowing a second note. The fancy wooden cuckoo call, a popular novelty, was fashioned in a variety of ways. The whole whistle might be shaped as a bird, or only the top section, or a carved and painted, or moulded, bird would be affixed to the body. Quite a number appear on the market from continental Europe, the country of origin occasionally identifiable by a word or two written on the call. Ceramic examples are illustrated under 'Ceramic whistles' (see pages 24, bottom, and 26, top).

There is a steady demand for whistles depicting animals and intended to be given as gifts, with a dog's head being by far the most popular representation. Other animals' heads portrayed include swans, ducks, horses and boars. There are probably one-off heads carved by individuals but this must have been a rare practice and research has supported the view that factories produced standard lines in not only metal and china, but also in horn, bone and ivory. In the case of cast-metal heads, specialist companies would supply manufacturers, who could then attach them to a variety of objects including whistles.

Whistles at work

Whistles have been used in many spheres of life and popular collecting areas include the armed services, the police, fire brigades, transport, sport, the Scouts and Guides and whistles for general public use and by industry.

Bosuns' calls are known from *c.*1500 and traditionally the various parts have been given nautical names: the *buoy* (the resonating chamber), the *gun* (the tube along which air is blown), the *keel* (the flat plate below the gun), and the *shackle* (the ring for a lanyard). The collector can discover silver examples with keels engraved with attractive designs, sometimes made by well-known silversmiths such as the Batemans, George Unite and Joseph Willmore, and by a major producer of the nineteenth century, Hilliard & Thomason of Birmingham. A rise in demand by navies at the end of the nineteenth century was met by J. Hudson & Co and A. De Courcy & Co, when engraved designs almost entirely gave way to die-stamped designs. Many calls issued by the Royal Navy were in nickel silver or plated brass with plain keels, and from the early twentieth century they bear the broad arrow mark. Presentation calls have been made in gold, hallmarked silver, silver-plated brass and in miniature sizes. The Motor Torpedo Boat Service was supplied from the 1900s with a composite whistle made up of a general service and a round pea whistle, the design registered by J. Hudson & Co in 1895. Whistles of this design were later made by W. Dowler & Sons and A. De Courcy & Co but are difficult to find.

The Rifle Brigade and light infantry regiments have whistles as part of their officers' equipment. An embossed lion's head, or regimental motif, set into a circular disc is attached by lengths of chain to the lanyard ring of a Beaufort whistle in a case, and both case and disc are affixed to a strap worn across the chest. The army used the round

J. Hudson & Co presentation whistles. (Left to right) Royal Marines Light Infantry, silver, 1922; 11th Devons, 9 carat gold, 1913; Cavalry Cup referee's whistle, silver, 1937.

Bosuns' calls. (Top, left to right) Hilliard & Thomason, silver, 1860; A. De Courcy & Co, patent 10035/1909. (Centre, left to right) George Unite, silver, 1907; J. Hudson & Co, silver US pattern, 1930s. (Bottom, left to right) E. Emanuel, silver, patent 7673/1896; J. Hudson & Co, 1920s.

whistle with a stop-hole from Victorian times and it had three different designs of top cap: with a knop, with a cap figured as a rose, and with concentric rings pressed into the cap. The general service whistle is used by many sections of the army and an enduring image is an officer in the trenches blowing his whistle during the First World War to command his men to 'go over the top'. The infantry whistle is a general service whistle attached to a leather thong and marked with the year of issue and/or a broad arrow mark. They are known with dates from 1889 to 1970, though not for every year and often without the thong. Later calls are marked with a stock number, typically '973 - 7001', and bear the broad arrow. For cavalry the whistle has a 30 mm (1¹/₄ inch) ring at the back, large enough to slip over a gloved finger. These are

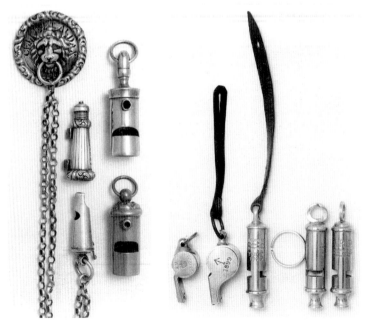

Far left: *(Left) Jennens & Co, King's Royal Rifle Corps officer's dress whistle, silver, 1865. (Right, top) Army whistle, late nineteenth century; (bottom) J. Hudson & Co army whistle with rose-figured top, 1910s.*

Left: *J. Hudson & Co. (Left to right) Second World War Royal Air Force air-crew whistle; artillery model; infantry model; cavalry model; air raid precautions whistle.*

much more uncommon and only a few years are known, the earliest recorded being 1908. Artillery was issued with the largest size escargot, body diameter 27 mm (1 inch), with a leather thong, and again not a common whistle when dated, 1899 being the earliest noted. From the early 1970s they have been marked with a broad arrow and a stock number, typically 'CN 973 - 6266'. Swagger sticks at around 610 mm (24 inches) usually consist of a round pea or general service whistle at the end of a cane either partially or wholly covered in brown or black leather. RAF air-crew during the Second World War were issued with a small escargot with a tapering mouthpiece, one side of the body marked '293/14/L1795', the other with 'A.M. [crown symbol] 23/230'. The RAF police use general service whistles which once were marked with a stock code that included 'AM', for 'Air Ministry', but since the 1950s includes '23' instead. A historically interesting whistle is that issued for air-raid precautions during the Second World War. It is marked 'ARP' and is one of the most common of all whistles as huge numbers were fabricated and distributed throughout Britain.

The Thames Marine Police had bosuns' calls at the end of the

J. Hudson & Co swagger sticks, longest 760 mm.

Left: *Police issue whistles. (Left to right) S. Auld, Glasgow Police, 'Police', late nineteenth century; J. Hudson & Co, 'Corporation of Glasgow Police Dept.', 1940s; J. Hudson & Co, 'Metropolitan Police', first issue with number engraved down the back, 1884; W. Dowler & Sons, 'Leeds Police', late nineteenth century; Smith & Wright, 'Liverpool Police', late nineteenth century.*

Below: *A. C. Riome truncheon with whistle, registered design 604460/1912.*

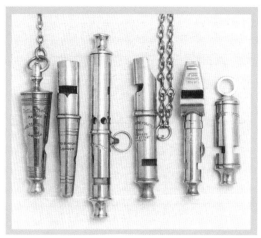

J. Hudson & Co. (Left to right) Fire brigade issue 'The King's Whistle', 'Shand Mason & Co', late 1880s; fire brigade issue, 'Shand Mason & Co London', 1900s; composite signal horn and general service whistle, c.1925; Motor Torpedo Boat Service whistle with 1000 mm 'gunner's chain', 1910s; composite 'Acme City' and 'Acme Thunderer', 1950s; oval 'Metropolitan'.

eighteenth century and city police used whistles from around the 1820s. Originally they were not an item issued to every officer but were kept for special situations. Today these early whistles are unidentifiable as they do not have any special markings. From the 1860s police forces began to equip all officers. The Liverpool Police were equipped with Beaufort whistles probably made by Thomas Yates and, during the 1880s and 1890s, by W. Dowler & Sons, J. Hudson & Co and J. Barrall. The police whistle, the general service whistle, has been made since the 1860s. Early makers include J. Stevens & Sons, W. Dowler & Sons and Bent & Parker. J. Hudson & Co, formed in 1870, made a pattern of general service whistle that was issued to Metropolitan Police officers in 1884, bearing their company address of the time, '84 Buckingham St'. Most other forces soon chose the 'Metropolitan' but there were exceptions. For example, Glasgow Police chose various whistle patterns, firstly round pea whistles made by S. Auld of Glasgow, then c.1920 the 'Metropolitan' and finally Hudson's escargot, the 'Acme Thunderer'. Generally whistles issued to police are marked with the force's name.

Railway whistles. (Top, from left) A. De Courcy & Co 'GWR Loco Dept 2353', late 1900s; North Eastern Railway station-master's whistle, 'NER'; J. Hudson & Co North Staffordshire Railway, branded 'NSR', horn, 1920s; J. Hudson & Co taxi-call model 'LNER', 1930s; J. Hudson & Co 'LMS' pressed whistle with under-strengthening, 1940s. (Bottom, from left) W. Kurath, Flums, Switzerland, Swiss Federal Railways, 'SBB CFF' ('Schweizerische Bundesbahnen/ Chemins de Fer Fédéraux Suisses'); Thomas Yates North Eastern Railway, 'NER', 1870s.

Above: *Sports whistles. (Top, left to right) J. Hudson & Co multi-tube, 1960s; J. Hudson & Co, Bakelite, 1930s; J. Hudson & Co, 'Tornado', plastic, 1990s; J. Hudson & Co, 'Acme Cyclone 888', plastic, late 1990s. (Bottom, left to right) M. Y. Dart & Co 'Halex', 1970s; J. Hudson & Co, plastic, 1960s; A. De Courcy & Co 'Abbey Referee', late 1910s.*

Above: *J. Hudson & Co transport whistles. (Top) Glasgow City Transport, 'GCT', escargot with strengthened barrel-ends and toothgrips, 1930s; London Passenger Transport Board, 'LPTB', Bakelite, 1930s. (Bottom) Birmingham & Midlands Omnibus Co, 'BMMO', multi-tube with angled mouthpiece, 1950s.*

Right: *Scouts and Guides. (Top, from left) J. Hudson & Co fleur-de-lis registered design, 1910s; J. Hudson & Co 'The Acme Scout Master' with stophole, 1940s; J. Hudson & Co 'The Acme Scout' with compass top, made in three sizes, 1940s–60s; A. De Courcy & Co 'The Boy Scouts' with compass attached to the body, made in three sizes, registered design 700191/1923. (Bottom, from left) J. Hudson & Co 'Girl Guides', 1930s; J. Hudson & Co 'The Acme Boy Scouts', 1930s; J. Hudson & Co knife whistle 'The Acme Boy Scouts', 1930s; A. De Courcy & Co, top shaped as a Scout's hat, made in three sizes, registered design 553181/1909.*

To summon assistance a policeman sounded three sharp blasts, but from the late 1960s their everyday use came to an end with the introduction of personal radios. The prisons service uses the general service whistle but it is rare for them to be marked with the name of an establishment. J. Hudson & Co produced an oval 'Metropolitan' which was advertised

Small low-pressure whistles for air and steam applications, longest 54 mm.

as being particularly suitable for female prison warders. General service whistles marked with the names of asylums and mental hospitals are known from the 1880s to the 1930s.

Calls manufactured for fire brigade use can be found from the 1880s to the 1920s. They include the general service whistle, a variety of composite whistles, and the 100 mm (4 inch) 'The King's Whistle' made by Hudson's. All firemen's calls are rare, with the rarest being those marked with the name of a brigade. More usually they are stamped with the name of a supplier of firefighting equipment: Merryweather & Sons, Shand Mason & Co, J. Morris & Sons and Rose & Co.

Railway personnel have utilised several models over a long period. It is judged that the earliest, pre-1870, were Beaufort and round pea patterns. Those of particular interest to collectors are marked with the initials of railway companies and, towards the end of the nineteenth century, included round pea whistles made of horn. Probably a number of companies made horn whistles but only two can be identified with any certainty, Hill Bros of Sheffield and J. Hudson & Co. Volume production of escargots first commenced around the 1880s. These were made for the railways by Black & Co (retailed by McPherson Brothers), A. De Courcy & Co, J. Hudson & Co, P. McDonald and H. A. Ward. In 1923 the railway companies were amalgamated into four groups, the Great Western Railway, the London Midland & Scottish Railway, the London & North Eastern Railway and the Southern Railway, and in 1947 they were nationalised, becoming British Railways (BR).

City tramway escargots were frequently of a robust construction, having extra metal plates to the sides and marked with sets of initials ending with the letter 'T', for 'Tramways' or 'Transport'. London Transport often used Bakelite escargots with company initials either marked directly into the body or on an inset metal plate. The Automobile Association favoured a small escargot marked on the mouthpiece 'A.A' and the Royal Automobile Club had a general service whistle with a monogram. Pedal cyclists purchased mouth whistles before bells became widely adopted at the end of the nineteenth century. A much sought-after whistle, 'The Cyclists Road Clearer', was made by J. Stevens & Sons (retailed by H. A. Knox & Co) and by J. Hudson & Co, both having a spherical top as originally designed by Porteous.

Cyclists' whistles. (Left to right) A. De Courcy & Co (?) spherical whistle with spoked wheel sides, c.1900; J. Hudson & Co 'The Cyclists Own', 1900s; J. Hudson & Co 'The Cyclists Road Clearer', late 1890s.

The referee's whistle, once metal or Bakelite but then often made of various types of plastic, is attached to the person with a lanyard or with finger-grips, an attachment at the base of the call allowing it to be slipped over fingers. A popular whistle at the start of the twenty-first century has an escargot's shape but operates in a different way. When blown, it does not convulse a pea within a chamber but instead sounds two or three pealess chambers formed within a moulding. What would have been the sides of the chamber in a traditional escargot now function only as a place to grip the whistle. Referees did not always use an escargot; in the 1920s general service whistles were sold marked 'The Referee'. Short, tapering calls with a finger-ring fixed underneath were marketed as suitable for referees in the 1930s. Multi-tube whistles were also popular. These consisted of several tubes, normally two but up to four, joined to a single mouthpiece.

The Scouts have had general service whistles since 1909, and the Guides from 1923. Originally the largest call was for Scout Masters, the next size for Guide Mistresses and Boy Scouts, and the smallest for Girl Guides. A. De Courcy & Co's range included in 1909 three sizes with a top shaped as a Scout's hat. They made a range with a compass attached to the side of the body, a design which Hudson's used after buying them out in 1927. In 1924 Hudson's made five sizes in which the top cap was replaced with a compass. Their inexpensive 'Emca' ('Acme' in reverse) range of whistles was made between the 1920s and 1940s marked in various ways, with 'Boy Scouts', 'Be Prepared' and the fleur-de-lis symbol. There were whistles with penknives: De Courcy's 'Scout Knife Whistle' hinged at the mouthpiece, Hudson's 'The Acme Boy Scouts' hinged at the top. Hudson's produced several escargots with a compass set in the side and although they were aimed at the Scouts they were not marked as such. They made several attractive whistles especially for the Scouts: one shaped as a fleur-de-lis, a long flat whistle with a compass and stop-hole, and a flat whistle with a stop-hole.

Above left: *Thomas Yates. Late-nineteenth-century patterns in brass and Britannia metal, some impressed 'TY' or 'T. Yates'.*

Above right: *J. Dixon & Sons. Late-nineteenth-century patterns in Britannia metal, ivory, nickel silver and horn.*

Left: *J. Hudson & Co. (Top, left to right) Escargot with a lip to the bottom of the mouthpiece; escargot with a lip to the top and bottom of the mouthpiece; tapered escargot, made in three sizes; escargot with compass, made in three sizes. (Bottom) 'Acme Thunderer' shaped as a First World War tank; round pea whistle, 1920s; round pea whistle, 1890s; round pea whistle made to patent 435/1885. The mouthpiece shape indicates it was made by James Hudson himself, co-founder of J. Hudson & Co.*

Below: *J. Hudson & Co escargots. (Top, from left) 'Rose' registered design 576579/1911; 'Shamrock' registered design 578510/1911; 'Thistle' registered design 577844/1911; 'The Acme JHCo England' made in four sizes, 1930s. (Centre, from left) 'The Acme Thunderer' made in three sizes in several colours, marked 'Acmeoid' (Bakelite) on the under side, 1910s 30c; 'Acme' made in black and brown in two sizes, plastic, patent 447673/1936; 'Acme', made in several colours, plastic, patent 620720/1949. (Bottom, from left) Nickel-plated antimonal lead, patent 447673/1936; 'The Acme Thunderer' made in three sizes with parallel-sided mouthpiece, tapered from the 1940s; 'The Acme Thunderer' with dog's-head barrel-end; 'The Acme Thunderer', made in three sizes, patent 19868/1891.*

Above left: *J. Hudson & Co plastics. (Left to right) Mottled blue thermo-plastic, 1960s; walnut Bakelite, 1910s; black plastic 'Acme'; green multi-tube with angled mouthpiece, 1950s; walnut Bakelite 'Metropolitan', 1930s; white 'Acme City', registered design 845440/1945; dark brown Bakelite, 1910s.*

Above right: *R. Perry & Co 'Perry Whistle', plastic, 1980s, length 89 mm.*

Left: *(Top) J. Stevens & Sons 'Porteous's Whistle' on an overlabel, pre-1870. (Bottom, from left) S. Auld 'Improved Call', registered design 143091/1890; R. A. Walton 'The Rattler', 1900s; Black & Co 'The Thunderer', 1890s.*

(From left) Whistles by J. Barrall, 1886–98: round pea; escargot, 'Barrall Birmingham'; Beaufort, 'Liverpool City Police'; general service whistle, 'London City Police Barrall Birmingham'. Whistles by Coney & Co, 1900s: general service whistle 'Coney's Alarm'; pea whistle.

21

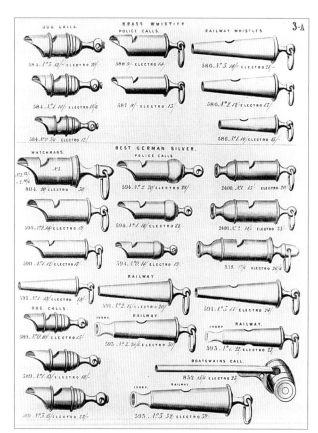

Thomas Yates. Page 3A of their c.1870 catalogue.

J. Hudson & Co. Selection of small patterns, longest 69 mm. The whistle on the left, engraved 'Engelberg 1914', was one of several made to be given away to acquaintances by the Hudson family whilst on holiday.

Right: *A. De Courcy & Co manufactured whistles from 1888 to 1927. (Top, left to right) Round pea whistle; escargot 'The Thunderer', made to patent 26019/1905; multi-tube with in-line mouthpiece; composite whistle; pressed escargot; round pea whistle. (Bottom, left to right) Fancy round pea whistle, registered design 158176/1890; Beaufort whistle, sometimes marked 'The Assistance'.*

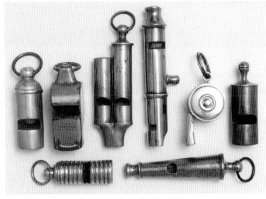

Below: *Smith & Wright whistles of the 1890s.*

Organisations and institutions would have their own name applied to whistles, as would companies including gentlemen's outfitters, sporting goods suppliers and hardware shops. During the first half of the twentieth century members of the public were tempted with a large range of calls made by different manufacturers. Some were plain; some bore trademarks such as 'Metropolitan' or 'Acme Thunderer'; others had marketing names such as 'City Police or Fire Whistle', 'Assistance', 'Rattler' and 'Universal'.

'Button whistles', made from tinplate curved around buttons to form an escargot, were made during the nineteenth and early twentieth centuries. They form a wide and interesting group and were produced using tunic buttons from, for example, the Pilot Boat Service, the Prisons Department, fire services, the General Post Office, railway companies, police forces, liverymen and army regiments.

'Button whistles'. (Top, left to right) Trinity Light House Service; fire service; Bradford Borough Police. (Centre, left to right) Great Eastern Railway; Prisons Department. (Bottom, left to right) Light Infantry; livery-button whistle; General Post Office.

(From left)
Pearlware, c.1830;
pearlware, c.1820;
Pratt ware, c.1790;
marbled clay, early
nineteenth century;
creamware, early
nineteenth century.

Ceramic whistles

Ceramic whistles have been made in many parts of the world for many hundreds of years. Pieces collectors are most likely to discover are generally from the end of the eighteenth century onwards. In Britain, from the 1760s to the 1830s, several ceramic bodies and decorating styles particular to the period were employed. Sought-after types are creamware, Pratt ware and pearlware. Creamware, a cream-coloured earthenware from the 1760s, was first produced in commercial quantities by Wedgwood, but soon copied by others. Pratt ware, *c.*1790–1830, is a white or pale cream pottery decorated from a palette of blue, orange, green, yellow, black and brown. Pearlware, a body whiter than creamware, was developed by Wedgwood in the late 1770s. Pottery birds in nests, on branches and by themselves were made by country potteries during the second half of the nineteenth century. Whistles made in agate ware and slipware can be found. Agate ware is formed by folding together different coloured clays, giving the appearance of marbling. Slipware is earthenware decorated with clay, of a creamy consistency, applied over the piece.

Continental hard-paste porcelain was made throughout the nineteenth century but whistles date mostly from 1880 to 1910. Many models are known, such as birds, Mr Punch, clowns, frogs, babies in shoes and various figures. Westerwald, in the Rhineland, made grey stoneware models of birds, some requiring water to operate correctly, decorated in cobalt blue and manganese brown, from the nineteenth to the twentieth century. Continental mugs, cups and saucers with a bird whistle on

(Clockwise from left) Lancashire slipware, nineteenth century; Buckley pottery, c.1880; Sussex ware, marbled clay, second half of nineteenth century.

Left: *Continental hard-paste porcelain, 1880–1910.*

Below: *Continental souvenir ware with bird-whistle handles made for the British market, 1890–1900. (Back, from left) Cup and saucer, 'Think of Me'; mug, 'A Present from Scarborough'; mug with scene of houses and yachts. (Front, from left) Mug, 'The Wish Tower Eastbourne'; mug, 'Think of Me'.*

Below: *Novelty mugs with whistles on the handles. (From left) Japanese, 'Whistle for Your Milk', late twentieth century; Japanese, 'Whistle for Your Milk', cow with wobbly plastic eyes, late twentieth century; Shorter & Son, 'Sing a Song of Sixpence', 1930s.*

Left: *Selection of continental figures in red and white clay, c.1900. Height of policeman 72 mm.*

Westerwald, Rhineland, grey stoneware decorated in blue and brown, mid nineteenth to twentieth century.

the handle were imported into Britain between *c*.1890 and the 1920s as holiday souvenirs, many bearing the name of a resort and a coloured view, others with a pithy saying. The Staffordshire company Shorter & Son marketed a pottery mug in the 1930s with a bird whistle on a branch-shaped handle, the body embossed with a scene depicting 'Sing a Song of Sixpence'. Late-twentieth-century ceramic mugs include tankards from Korea with the inscription 'Whistle For Your Beer', and from Japan, 'Whistle For Your Milk', with embossed scenes depicting teddy bears, birds and cows' heads with wobbly plastic eyes.

There are small continental figures in red, and occasionally white,

Late-twentieth-century pottery tankards. The one on the right was made in Korea.

Crested souvenir ware. (From left) Mug for the Isle of Man, made in Bohemia, 1890–1900; jug for the City of London, made by Gemma, 1920s; water whistle, modelled as a Norwich warbler for Felixstowe, made by Arcadian, 1910–25.

Eggcups incorporating whistles, intended for confectionery, 1920–50.

clay from *c*.1900 depicting cattle, hares, dogs, men, women, children, owls, policemen, pixies, chickens and bears. Crested china with whistles includes a warbler by Arcadian made between 1910 and 1925, a jug by Gemma from the 1920s, and a mug, 'Made in Bohemia', 1890 to 1900. Between the 1920s and 1950s eggcups, presumably intended for an Easter confection, were modelled with a figure supporting or pulling the cup. Many are in orange lustre and marked 'Foreign', and patterns include ocean liners, ducks, chickens, policemen, locomotives, elephants, dogs, bears and motor cars. Ceramic whistles have been manufactured throughout the twentieth century by factories and studio potters alike, birds being a popular theme. Dog-headed whistles are illustrated under 'Whistles in the Countryside' (see page 11).

Novelty and toy whistles

Whistles have been incorporated into a number of different objects of varying usefulness. Members of the public could purchase in 1868 a Beaufort whistle made by Thomas Yates which had as a mouthpiece a carriage key. Coney & Co of Birmingham produced a carriage key hinged within a tube which could be unscrewed and which tapered at both ends, one of which formed a whistle; an alternative pattern contained a corkscrew. Some multi-bladed penknives of the nineteenth century have a whistle, as do items for châtelaines, such as a penknife–pencil–whistle arrangement or simply a mechanical pencil with a whistle end. This last item includes a model by the famous maker S. Mordan & Co. From 1905 A. De Courcy & Co offered general service whistles with penknives, as did J. Hudson & Co from 1907. Other novelties include

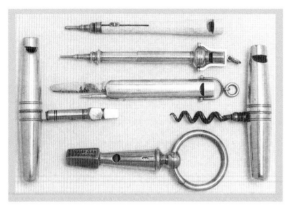

Left: *(Left) Coney & Co carriage key, 1900s. (Centre, top to bottom) Bone with retractable pencil; S. Mordan & Co mechanical pencil; S. McAdam & Co (?) silver penknife and retractable pencil; Thomas Yates carriage key, registered design 1868. (Right) Coney & Co corkscrew, 1900s.*

Right: *Nineteenth-century European multi-bladed knife.*

Below: *(Left, top) Whistle and compass, silver, 1896; (bottom) 'Whistle and I'll come to you my lad', sterling silver. (Centre) Ring-whistle, silver. (Right, top) Whistle with compass and map scales; (bottom) Fabergé perfume bottle.*

magnetic compasses, rings, hairbrushes, watches, watch keys, perfume bottles and map measurers. Many small whistles in a wide range of qualities have been made for attachment to bracelets, key rings and neck chains. As well as the preferred whistle alloys, brass and nickel silver, they can be found in gold, silver, bone and many minerals including jade, jasper, jet, agate, carnelian and bog-oak. Bog-oak is a form of oak preserved in peat deposits and became popular for black mourning jewellery following the death of Prince Albert in 1861. Once small objects were attached to watch-chains, including silver whistles and miniature bosuns' calls, and there is also a pocket-watch-shaped whistle. Souvenir whistles can be found in slate from Wales, in serpentine from Cornwall and at the end of Scottish horn spoons.

Above: Small whistles for attachment to bracelets and chains. (Top, from left) Black marble, length 52 mm; horn with brass fittings; agate; jade. (Bottom, from left) Whitby jet; carnelian seal with rotating wheel; jasper; bog-oak.

Above: *Small whistles for attachment to bracelets and chains. Length of shoe 25 mm.*

Right: *(Left) Two-tone whistle shaped like a pocket watch. (Right) Selection of watch-chain whistles, longest 45 mm: (from top) J. Hudson & Co engraved silver bosun's call; bosun's call, silver, maker's mark 'AS'; J. Hudson & Co, silver, 1909; silver, maker's mark 'WT', 1879 – when held between the thumb and forefinger the open-ended barrel becomes an effective resonating chamber.*

Scottish horn spoon with silver mounts, length 145 mm.

(Top, from left) Cigarette-holder case, silver, 1904; H. C. Butcher pipe tamper and cheroot pricker, patent 1166/1866; Alexander & James curved vesta, silver, 1835. (Centre, from left) French vesta with relief figure of a huntsman and dog, silver-plated; J. Hudson & Co cigar pricker, c.1900; engraved vesta, silver, 1884. (Bottom, from left) Continental Bakelite whistle and petrol lighter, showing cap removed; French 'whistle lamp', shown unscrewed – whistle, central fuel reservoir and wick, and top cap.

Souvenir whistles. (From left) Welsh slate; Cornish serpentine; Stanhope with a view of Interlaken, wood and fur; Stanhope with six views of Brighton, bone.

Smokers have been supplied with a number of requisites combined with whistles. There is from the 1930s a European petrol lighter with a Bakelite whistle depicting balloonists on the side. Cases for early friction matches, vestas, were made from the mid nineteenth century mostly in brass or silver. They often included a striker, which in English examples is usually down the body, and in French ones on the lid. Cigarette-holder cases with a whistle end were also made. In 1866 H. C. Butcher patented a spring-loaded cigar pricker combined with an ivory whistle and pipe tamper, and around 1900 J. Hudson & Co produced a cigar pricker and whistle. There are several designs of pipes with whistles, all working on the same basic principle. When the mouthpiece of the pipe is blown into, a valve closes the airway to the bowl and opens an airway to a whistle recessed in the stem

'Stanhopes', often called 'peepers', date principally from the 1890s and are commonly in horn and bone. These whistles have, set in the top, a lens and photographic transparency showing between one and twelve views.

Souvenir Mauchline ware is fine giftware, mostly in sycamore, made at Mauchline, Scotland, and at other locations from sometime before the 1850s until the 1930s. The two most common finishes are transfer and photographic ware. A transfer or photograph was applied to the wood and given several coats of clear varnish. Less common ranges are tartan, black lacquer, floral and fern ware. In tartan ware, the pattern is hand-painted on to the whistle or a machine-

Mauchline ware. (Left to right) Fern ware; transfer ware, 'The Harbour at St Heliers Jersey'; photographic ware, 'Blackgang Chine'; floral ware; black lacquer ware, 'From Brighton'; tartan ware, 'McBeth'.

Right: *Soot or flour whistles. The central cavity is filled with soot or flour and, if blown without depressing the end plunger, the powder is blown into the face. 1920s–30s.*

Below: *A selection of toy wooden whistles which have been produced over many years.*

Below: *(Left) French cast escargot with tasselled lanyard, Queen Victoria's Diamond Jubilee, 1897. (Right) J. Hudson & Co, George VI's coronation, black and red escargot with red, white and blue lanyard.*

produced paper design is applied. Floral patterns were applied to plain wood or black lacquered bodies. Fern ware, where real ferns or printed fern designs were used, seems to be the rarest type of Mauchline ware for whistles.

For Queen Victoria's Golden Jubilee silver escargot whistles were made from 1887 shillings by Thornton & Co of London, and for the 1897 Diamond Jubilee, French cast escargots. J. Hudson & Co made an inexpensive black and red

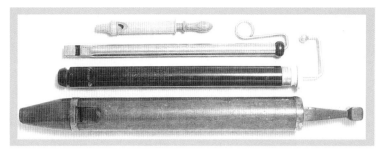

Above: *Slide whistles. (Top to bottom) Wooden; J. Hudson & Co 'The Acme Jazza', 1930s; S. B. Barnes 'Swanee Whistle', de luxe model with ivory top, registered design 1921; mahogany pitch pipe with brass mounts, the slide marked with the pitch on an inset lead strip, length 490 mm.*

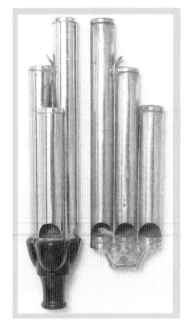

Left: *J. Hudson & Co. Multi-tube tug-boat effects whistles, longest 163 mm.*

plastic whistle with a red, white and blue lanyard for the coronation of King George VI in 1937.

Slide whistles have an internal plunger which may be moved up and down the body to change the pitch. They were used as sound effects instruments, variable pitchpipes, toys, bird calls and by jazz bands. Larger examples were used on car exhausts. The 'Swanee Whistle' by S. B. Barnes, a registered design of 1921, was available in at least five sizes. Since the 1920s J. Hudson & Co manufactured a range including 'The Acme Jazza' and the 'Kentucky Song Whistle'. Many others exist, from well-constructed metal patterns to throwaway plastic toys, as do other effects instruments.

'Penny toys' are small toys made between the 1890s and the 1930s intended to be sold for one old penny (1d). There are Japanese lithographed tinplate examples from the 1920s and 1930s, either sold as toys or put into festive crackers, along with slide, songster and cast-metal whistles. Cast French penny toys can be found in various alloys portraying many items including, birds, fish, balloons, locomotives, clocks, cars, pistols, whips, soda-water siphons, guitars, keys, aeroplanes, cannons and boats. Many bear the word 'Deposé' or 'France'. Occasionally the initials of the manufacturer appear, such as 'SR' for Simon & Rivollet or the unidentified manufacturers 'GFB', 'A & Ce' and 'CH & JU'.

Songster, warbler or water whistles are a large range of calls which need to be partially filled with water to operate correctly. Some are illustrated in the chapters on 'Whistles in the Countryside' (see page 10) and 'Ceramic Whistles' (see page 26, top). Many can be

F. L. Johnson effects whistle. The sound may be varied by squeezing the top rubber bole whilst blowing. US patent 396821/1889, length 68 mm.

Right: *Japanese tinplate whistles put in festive crackers and sold individually, 1920s–30s. Length of playing card 42 mm.*

Below left: *'Penny toys', 1890–1930s. (Clockwise from top left) Simon & Rivollet locomotive marked 'SR France', length 44 mm; Smith & Wright pistol, registered design 285956/1896; lamp, 'Déposé'; balloon; soda-water siphon, 'Déposé GFB'; domino, bone and wood; fish.*

Below right: *'Penny toys', 1890–1930s. (Clockwise from left) Whip, 'Déposé', length 75 mm; clock, 'Déposé'; fish; binoculars; guitar, 'Déposé'; pistol.*

Right: *Songster, or warbler, whistles that require partial filling with water to operate properly. The one at the top is by O. Schwarzkopf, US patent 1445362/1923, brass with moving beak and tail, height, without mouth-tube, 90 mm.*

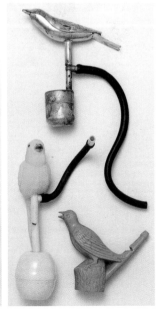

Right: Japanese tinplate whistles, 1950s–60s.

Bing model steam-engine whistle, length 35 mm.

found in metal and in plastic, both old and new. A sought-after songster is Schwarzkopf's 1923 US Patent 1445362, made in brass with the top modelled as a bird. Blowing it causes the tail and beak to move. Whistles married with rattles and teethers are mostly from the Victorian era onwards; those from the eighteenth century are uncommon and command high prices. The word 'plastic' encompasses an assortment of synthetic materials including celluloid, Bakelite and vinyl. They have been used for both high-quality and inexpensive whistles, and the number of different toys and novelties is huge, from conventionally shaped whistles to complex arrangements embracing many classifications of objects and animals.

Below: *Plastic toys. (Clockwise from top left) J. & L. R. Ltd penny-farthing cycle, 1950s, length 103 mm; ocean liner; Kleeware locomotive, 1960s; dark green locomotive, 1950s; J. & L. R. Ltd motor-cyclist, 1950s; Fairylite pistol; green dog's head; Palitoy general service whistle.*

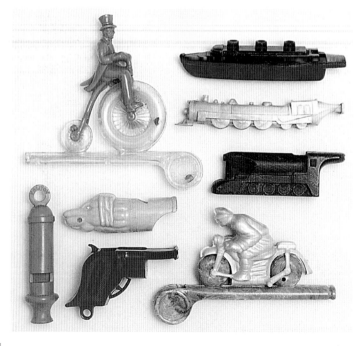

Airfix clockwork whistling boy, 1950s, height 240 mm.

Above: *(Top) Plastic slide whistle with cat, cello and bird. (Bottom) Combex plastic slide whistle, registered design 881470/1956, length 210 mm.*

Below left: *Rattles and teethers. (Clockwise from left) Vegetable ivory with five metal bells, length 180 mm; black wooden ball containing a bell, with ivory whistle and ring; silver rattle and mother-of-pearl teether, 1861; Adie & Lovekin silver rattle and coral teether, 1906; silver and mother-of-pearl teether, 1844.*

Right: *Ideal Toy Corporation 'Mr Machine' clockwork whistling toy, US patent 3763734/1973, height 450 mm.*

Larger whistles

Most speaking-tubes consist of a removable whistle fitted into the centre of a mouthpiece and connected to a similar arrangement by tubing. From the 1860s until the 1920s many patents were taken out relating to them. They enabled passengers to speak to the driver of an omnibus, tram or cab at a time when he sat apart in the open. The system was also used in luxury cars between the passengers and the chauffeur. At one time the only rapid way of communicating within mansions, trains and ships was by speaking-tubes. Where they were installed throughout a large building, for example, and terminated at a single place, the whistles were fitted with indicators. An indicator is a long peg recessed in the centre of the whistle, or a hinged flap on the side. The peg shot forward, or the flap dropped down, when the caller blew, thus indicating amongst a group of whistles which one to respond to. Speaking-tube whistles and mouthpieces are found in ivory, bone, plastic and a variety of woods including lignum vitae, with the visible tubing covered with coloured braiding. For nautical use they were made in plated or unplated brass, and in some applications the whistle and mouthpiece were set into a hinged lid attached to a bell-shaped tube-ending. When the lid was lifted the operator could, if necessary, shout down the bell-end. In early trains a speaking-tube was fitted between the locomotive's footplate and

Above: *J. Hudson & Co speaking-tube with wooden whistle and mouthpiece with brass fittings, one of a pair for omnibus use, overall length 610 mm; ivory whistle and mouthpiece; 'Whishaw's Improved Telekouphonon' Bakelite whistle with bone indicator.*

Right: *Speaking-tube with mouthpieces and whistles. Length overall 3200 mm.*

Marine speaking-tube mouthpieces with whistles. The largest example shows a flap 'indicator' and a hinged bell-end, height 230 mm.

the guard's van at the rear. For passengers' use each coach was connected to the guard's van.

Bicycles were fitted with mechanically blown whistles made to various patent designs of the 1880s to the 1900s. Some had a pair of bellows, or a piston, which would supply air when activated by lowering a drive wheel on to a tyre, or a belt on to a spindle. E. H. Morgan's patent of 1892 relied on the vibration of the saddle to compress air into a reservoir. There were a number of patterns which were based on a whistle with a squeezable bulb attached to the handlebars. Motor vehicle whistles were not generally operated by a squeezable bulb but were blown with exhaust or cylinder-head gases. The whistles came with a valve

(Left to right) Lancashire & Yorkshire Railway steam locomotive whistle, marked 'L & Y RLY', height 245 mm; triple-chime steam whistle; typical simple steam whistle.

37

Car cylinder-head whistles. R. D. Buell, Chicago, USA, 'Explosion Whistle', US patent 1252232/1918; G. F. Hall, Newark, USA, 'Ideal', US patent 1327323/1920.

Right: Car exhaust whistles. (Top) A. H. Treloggan 'The Stentophone', patent 14282/1912. (Centre) M & B 'Nightingale' slide whistle, registered design 307255/1897. (Bottom) S. D. Mitchell 'Chantecler', patent 21736/1911.

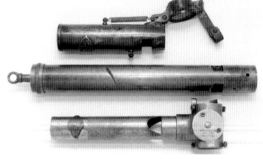

Left: Vehicle exhaust whistles. (Top) Randall-Faichney Co, Boston, USA, 'Jericho' car whistle, US patent 1031678/1912. (Centre) Lee Tire & Rubber Co, Conshohocken, USA, 'The Waymaker' car whistle, 1910s. (Bottom) Esco motorcycle whistle, 1910s.

from which ran a wire to a foot-pedal or hand-lever. A number of exhaust models consisted of several whistles mounted together or were of the variable-pitch slide type. For motorcyclists there were exhaust patterns operated by a foot-pedal, though a small-size 'Chantecler' advertised by Brown Brothers of London in 1913 was hand-controlled.

The largest whistles are those that have been used by factories, steam cranes, traction engines, locomotives and ships. They have been used

Left: *Steam whistle and valve. Overall height 370 mm.*

Right: *Triple-chime steam locomotive whistle. South African Railways, marked 'SAS' and 'SAR', height 360 mm.*

Left: *Crosby, USA, triple-chime ship's steam whistle, 1900s. Height 500 mm, weight 16 kg.*

Right: *W. H. Bailey ship's steam whistle, patent 1706/1873. Height 500 mm, weight 9 kg.*

for both signalling and warning. Smaller sizes were part of steam-boiler warning systems or were used as signals at factories and shipyards. Sought by collectors are those from steam locomotives with railway company markings, each company having its own preferred whistle shape. The largest steam whistles were those used by ships and can weigh as much as 340 kg (750 pounds) – of *Titanic* proportions!

Further reading

Baker, John. *Mauchline Ware*. Shire Publications, reprinted 1998.
Bracegirdle, Cyril. *Collecting Railway Antiques*. Patrick Stephens, 1988.
Dike, Catherine. *Cane Curiosa*. Dike, Geneva, 1983.
Dundas, James L. *Collecting Whistles*. Schiffer Publishing, Atglen, 1995. (A USA perspective.)
Gilchrist, Martyn, and Topman, Simon. *Collecting Police Whistles and Similar Types*. Topcrest, 1998.
Pressland, David. *The Book of Penny Toys*. New Cavendish Books, 1991.

PERIODICALS
The annual publication *Miller's Collectables Price Guide* has illustrated a number of whistles over the years. Early motor trade magazines, many illustrating whistles for vehicles, can be found in the library of the National Motor Museum, Beaulieu, Hampshire SO42 7ZN. Telephone: 01590 612345. Website: www.beaulieu.co.uk

Places to visit

It is always advisable to check opening times and to find out what items are on display.

Greater Manchester Police Museum, Newton Street, Manchester M1 1ES. Telephone: 0161 856 3287.
Horniman Museum, 100 London Road, Forest Hill, London SE23 3PQ. Telephone: 020 8699 1872. Website: www.horniman.demon.co.uk
Imperial War Museum, Lambeth Road, London SE1 6HZ. Telephone: 020 7416 5000. Website: www.iwm.org.uk
Kelham Island Museum, Alma Street, off Corporation Street, Sheffield S3 8RY. Telephone: 0114 2722106. Website: www.simt.co.uk (Collection of J. Dixon & Sons whistles.)
National Army Museum, Royal Hospital Road, Chelsea, London SW3 4HT. Telephone: 020 7730 0717. Website: www.national-army-museum.ac.uk
National Maritime Museum, Greenwich, London SE10 9NF. Telephone: 020 8858 4422. Website: www.nmm.ac.uk
West Midlands Police Museum, Sparkhill Police Station, Stratford Road, Sparkhill, Birmingham B11 4EA. Telephone: 0121 626 7181. Website: www.stvincent.ac.uk/Resources/WMidPol

Eggcups with whistles, intended for confectionery, 1920–50.